# Concentrated Blackness: An Inward-looking Solution to the Plight of Americanized Africans

Marcus M. Johnson, Jr.

Concentrated Blackness: An Inward-looking
Solution to the Plight of Americanized
Africans

*This is written out of love for the Americanized African, not out of any ill will toward the benefactors and beneficiaries of White Privilege.* – Marcus

# TABLE OF CONTENTS

# Part 1: The Situation

Americanized Africans -- commonly known as African Americans or Black people -- will never be viewed as equals in America. Although this country was built upon our ancestors, we will never be welcomed at the table. Although the government appears to care and pass laws to protect us, there will never be a law that specifically targets the white privilege that is at the root of most of our problems. We are underemployed and are disallowed by law from the easiest routes to entrepreneurship. The most profitable industries in the world

8

exploit our bodies but we are limited in the use of our own bodies for our own profit. Even the news profits from reporting the misery of our neighborhoods.

Lynching is not dead. It has just become a perk for white men and honorary white men who wear blue. The police do protect and serve, just not Americanized Africans and our communities. They are actually akin to the patrollers that were used to return Black people to slavery, during and after the institution was supposedly abolished.

9

Slavery is not dead.  It has just

evolved into a different kind of slavery.

Actually, if you really think about it, can

you honestly say that chattel slavery has

really ended?  How many Americanized

Africans are serving life sentences, right

now?  What were their crimes?  Were these

crimes of greed or crimes driven by need?

How many corporate or private prisons exist

in this country, today?  How much funding

do these prisons receive per capita?  Are

their slaves not transferred from prison to

prison, along with their associated funding?

10

When they leave the prison system, they remain forever connected to it, if only by their criminal records. This is the lifelong bondage and reduction of human life to property that separate chattel slavery from any other kind.

Americanized Africans, America owes you more than it can ever pay. If you all traced your lineage back to its last American slave, calculated the value of 40 acres and mule, calculated the interest that would have accrued between then and now, you would find a number that this country could not pay.  If you could find some way to create a number that represents what was lost when our first enslaved ancestors were imported, you would likely have an equally unfathomable number that could not be paid.

It is time to stop being so loyal to a country that does not love us as much as it loves what we can do for it.  It is time to build and support our own, at all levels.  We should not be governed by those who cannot relate to our living conditions.  We should not be financially supporting outsiders.  We should not be monitored by people from outside of our communities. It is time to build our own, from the ground. Where is your money? Is it deposited in Bank of America or some other major bank with lending practices that have historically put funding out of your and your people's reach? Withdraw it and find a Black-owned credit union or a Black-owned bank. If there is none, research starting one.

Where do you shop for food and clothing? Is it another store owned by an immigrant who received a federal grant for which you would not be permitted to apply?

Stop shopping there. Make a list of Black-owned grocers, clothing stores, etc. and commit to supporting them in the same way that you would any other business. Stop asking for freebies and discounts at our businesses. Black business owners, stop offering subpar service, when you can afford to do better.

Who are you voting for? Republicans? Democrats? Both take us for granted. One assumes that we will never vote for them and the other that we will never not vote for them. Are you not voting

at all?  You are part of the problem.  We
need to create our own party.  Do not tell
believe that is cannot be done.  Do you
know who Fannie Lou Hamer is and what
the Mississippi Democratic Freedom Party
is?

Who is policing our neighborhoods?
We cannot let our own misfits overrun it,
but we cannot afford to rely on blue
domestic terrorists either.  Everyone who is
eligible, should go to your local courthouse,
register for your weapons license, and invest
in a shotgun and handgun.  If you are denied

your right to register to vote or carry a firearm, seek out others in a similar predicament and file a lawsuit. The ACLU will take the case.

It is time that we start planning and acting, instead of just discussing and fussing. Assemble your neighborhood militias, let the neighborhood know, and extend the invitation for others to join. There should not be any police activity in our neighborhoods that is not subject to the oversight of these militias. Are you mad about your schools? Tell your children to come back home and teach in them, after they graduate college. Build your own schools. We cannot rely on the oppressors to liberate us through education.

Pool your financial power, your political power, and your intellectual power. Our civic organizations are dead. The NAACP and others are a joke. The church should be the nucleus for such an operation but they have become more business than community service oriented and thus more useful to sustain the current system than correcting its issues. We may need to rethink that relationship, also. We need to either redesign existing platforms for change or create new ones, if we want to survive and progress in "Egypt".

If you are thinking of doing nothing, remember just a few of the names among which you could easily be listed, if these conditions are allowed to persist.

- Sandra Bland – guilty of being Black and having self-esteem and self-respect

- Amadou Diallo – guilty of being Black in New York
- Eric Garner – guilty of past aspirations of entrepreneurship and of being Black in New York
- Freddy Gray – deprived of due process
- Trayvon Martin – guilty of walking while Black
- Tamir Rice – guilty of playing in a park while Black

19

- Walter Scott – guilty of being justifiably afraid while Black

- Alton Sterling – guilty of Black entrepreneurship

Inactivity is the equivalent of hanging yourself or another one of your sisters and brothers. The remainder of this book aims to help Black America remedy these issues and more.

# Part 2: The Solution

The presidency of Barack Obama left many people feeling that we had arrived at the post-race America of which many have long dreamed. However, the emergence of entities that include the Tea Party and presidential candidates like Donald Trump and Ted Cruz, as well as the resurgence of White Nationalism, police brutality directed toward Black people, and the justice and judicial systems endorsement of some of these entities via their inaction has revealed that we were just temporarily on the euphoric side of our cyclical history.

23

A Black president, Black PhDs and EdDs, Black politicians, and Black professionals across all industries have not resulted in that ideal post-race America. We are still haunted by the ghosts that laid the foundation of this nation.

In response to what appears to be the resurgence of hate in America, people have taken to the streets, destroyed life and property, and taken many other actions to remedy our race problem. However, they are lacking a well-thought, balanced plan.

They are also targeting a symptom and not the root cause.

What is this root cause? There are actually several. The bedrock issue is the unresolved history of American chattel slavery, which has grown into an unchecked mutant racism and the entrenched power structure that supports it. While this is an issue that must be handled by all Americans, there is an approach that Black people can take that does not rely on the cooperation of white America. This solution is an inward-looking approach with ambitions of

developing a greater degree of
independence. H ow can we demand
anything from the system upon which we
depend so heavily?  That is the near
equivalent of a child throwing a tantrum and
making demands of their parents.

Black America has to regain the
momentum that was lost with the advent of
integration.  The way we accomplish this is
through cooperative segregation.
Cooperative segregation is a state in which
our community takes care of itself and meets
other communities at market for trade

purposes. Cooperative segregation focuses on consolidating power and resources in the following 3 areas:

- Finance
- Geography
- Politics

## *Finances*

The first area upon which Black America needs to focus is finance. Right now, we invest in the very system that victimizes us. The majority of our money is invested in the major banks, banks that are far less likely to provide our people with personal loans, mortgages, small business loans, etc. We also spend the majority of our money with businesses and corporations, and brands that are either not Black-owned or not interested in the health of the Black community. Black America has some of the greatest spending power but the least wealth.

This is likely because we have a

misunderstanding of what wealth is. This is

also likely because we do not fully support

businesses that are owned by our

communities. We must divest and disinvest

in the system. We must invest in our own

and create a Black dollar.

The first step to creating a Black

dollar is finding a Black-owned bank or

credit union. Almost every state has one or

the other. If your state has no Black-owned

banking option, start one. If you or your

children do not have a bank account, anywhere, open one. If you already have an account somewhere, you do not have to move all of your money but you should at least have a savings account with whatever Black bank is near you.

Right now, so many Black people flock toward payday loan businesses and often get caught in the vicious cycle of short-term predatory lending that our country and many individual states refuse to rein in. Imagine if you took a small personal loan and created a payday loan business of your own, but with more reasonable business rates. Imagine if you structured it as a lending club with a small monthly membership fee. This would allow you to lend at lower interest rates and still be profitable. Such a lending operation could easily grow into a bank for areas that do not already have Black-owned options.

The next step to creating a Black dollar is patronizing Black businesses. Patronage of Black businesses may be inconvenient, at times. We may even feel that the service is subpar. However, the ability to provide higher levels of service and offer service at more locations and during expanded hours is directly connected to patronage. We must stop walking into Black businesses and expecting hook-ups and freebies. We must stop treating Black businesses disrespectfully just because they are Black businesses.

All of the responsibility of supporting Black businesses does not fall upon the consumers though. Black business owners need to refrain from taking shortcuts. They should also take great pride in the appearance of their establishments and products. When something is out of order at a Black-owned business, including if there is a consumer disrespecting the establishment, we should be quick to provide feedback, but provide feedback with love and encouragement.

In addition to patronizing existing Black businesses, when need to fill the vacuum when there is a service need for which there is not a Black-owned solution. Look for innovative ways to do this. Imagine if our professional athletes stopped allowing themselves to be exploited, took

their endorsements, fan-bases, and wealth,

leaving to create their own leagues.

Another step to creating Black

currency is understanding the difference

between assets and liability.  Although the

coiner escapes me, there is a phrase that

explains the difference.  The saying states,

"If it's on your ass, it's not an asset."  This

may be difficult to understand but clothes

are not an investment.  They do not

appreciate in value or even hold value.  The

same goes for vehicles, unless they are

antiques.  Things that lose value are

liabilities.

Mark your page and google Bill

Gates or Warren Buffett, really quick.  Then

click on "images".  For the most part, what

you will find are two very conservatively

dressed men, wearing clothing for which

you will likely have difficulty identifying

the brand.  These are two of the wealthiest

people in America.  Keep those images in

your head, the next time you drive around

poverty-stricken or lower middle class

neighborhoods and examine what your

neighbors may be wearing.  This illustrates the difference between wealth and stuff.

Wealth and financial concentration is just one piece in the puzzle that is the cooperative segregation that will allow Black people to live independent of the system that victimizes many of us.  Another piece to the puzzle is geographic.

### *Geography*

Find historic examples of great empires that were spread out and not vulnerable because of it.  The phenomenon is known is being over-extended or spread too thin. To help yourself better visualize it, imagine a basketball defensive set in which four players position themselves that the four corners of a basketball court and the fifth stand at center court. This would leave huge gaps that any recreation league team could exploit. If you are not sports savvy, pretend you are fixing a peanut butter and jelly sandwich and you are given half a teaspoon of peanut butter, half a teaspoon of jelly, and instructed to spread it evenly over two pieces of bread. You are going to have a disappointing PB&J sandwich. This a state similar to that of Black America. We are spread too far out. As a result of this, we can neither share resources nor protect each other.

We need to concentrate in geographic areas. Look for areas that are struggling and move there. Struggling areas are opportunities. As I peruse Facebook®, I often find friends who have thousands of Facebook® friends and acquaintances. How many of these friends live near you and are renting. You should be looking to build or purchase an apartment building or complex and all move in. Create an S corporation to protect your team from liability, purchase the properties through the business. You can set special rental rates for the members of the S corporation, and rent the remaining units at market rate.

If you and like-minded individuals more into the same communities, you can shape these communities. Create neighborhood watches or even small militias that police not only people but the police. There should be nothing out of the ordinary that happens in our communities and goes unnoticed. Even police activity should be monitored by community members.

These communities should also pursue ventures that produce food. Designate spaces for produce farming, and create farmers' markets. Picture a scenario in which people from outside of your community are coming to an open-air market for the produce that you have harvested. This is what cooperative segregation looks like, self-imposed isolation for health reasons, but meeting outsiders at the trading post.

Consolidating in a particular geographic area has clear implications for businesses and protection, but it also helps concentrate political power.

## *Politics*

All of the aforementioned areas are important; however, politics may be more important, when it comes to self-determinism and creating an identity that exists independent of the current abusive system, affording us a better chance at living and excelling. Concentrating in a common community helps to create stronger voting blocks. Unfortunately, the major parties resort to gerrymandering to dilute these blocks. A way to avoid this is to leave the major parties for a second-tier party with a platform that is more flexible, a party like the Green Party.

Would you give your body to someone, if they only did something to earn it, once every four years? Would you believe their concern and love was authentic and genuine, if it was only expressed leading

up to your quadrennial encounters? Would

you continuously throw yourself at someone

who did not want you? Would you feel

right wearing the chain, jacket, ring, or

badge of someone who constantly abused

you and whose rhetoric showed how little

they cared for you? If you had any sort of

pride, you would not. Unfortunately, there

are men and women who subject themselves

to these types of abusive relationships that

only benefit the abusers. American society,

particularly Black people and women, are in

comparable relationships with the major political parties of the United States of America – the Democratic and Republican parties. We continue to support parties which completely ignore or abuse us, until presidential election cycles. This is bananas! Many of us may feel hopeless, as if there is no other option. However, there is a viable option, a third party.

Throughout US political history, we have seen many parties come and go, Federalist, Antifederalists, Whigs, Mississippi Democratic Freedom Party, etc.

Some of these parties have endured, while many have simply faded for whatever reason. We have reach a crux where we need to resurrect or create more political parties. Why should we not stick beside the Democrats? They are doing nothing for us. This is the party that made no noise as the Voting Rights Act expired. There was no attempt to update and preserve the relevance of the Act that provided protections for every minority in America, including Black people and women. This is the party that spends little time visiting our hoods but likes

45

to blow kisses from afar or texts but never calls (the minimal needed to make some of us believe that they are interested in us). Why not the Republicans? Our support for them makes no since, unless we have "arrived" – using finances to emerge from the masses of the Black, poor, or vagina-bearing population segment or unless we can forget our people who have either died trying or continue to struggle in poverty.

We need to chuck the deuces and bid farewell to both of these plantations! Then there is the Libertarian Party which wants "minimum government" and "maximum freedom" per their website. They are just GOP, Jr. Lastly, we have the Green Party.

The Green Party (GP) is similar to what the Libertarian Party is for the Republican party, its platform aligns with the Democratic Party; however, they go even further to forward agendas that benefit the greater good of American society. The GP, not to be confused with the GOP (Grand Old Party, commonly known as the Republican Party), has 4 pillars and 10 key values. The pillars consist of peace,

47

ecology, social justice, and democracy.

Basically, this party wants us to stop killing

and dying in name of national defensive,

when it is really American Imperialism. The

GP wants us to protect our planet and treat it

as if we are not oblivious to the fact that we

do not have another planet to move to if we

finish destroying Earth. The party also

pushes for social impartiality and a real

democracy, not a system that has an

electoral college that can override popular

vote, if the popular vote and vote of the

powerful do not align. The 10 key values

align with the 4 pillars and include grassroots democracy, social justice and equal opportunity, ecological wisdom, non-violence, decentralization, community-based economics, feminism and gender equity, respect for diversity, personal and global responsibility, and future focus and sustainability.

In a nutshell, the Green Party is government for the people by the people (as the founders of the nation said they believed in), includes everyone without race- and gender-based discriminatory actions

49

(remember King, X, Evers, Anthony, Stanton, NAWSA, AWSA, Paul, and Burns), fosters a sense of global community instead of provoking countries and religions that do not align with mainstream American values.

Do we want government that values, respects, and protects us? Do we want government that values control by citizens and not the Koch brothers and businesses? Do we want logical actions and protection for things like ending the prohibition on marijuana, free healthcare and higher education, police oversight, fair wages and wage equality? If so, we do not want to support parties that are run by people who have already gotten what they need are minimally, if at all, concerned with the needs and quality of life of others.

You know how we incredulously look at people who remain in abusive relationships, especially those who keep waiting, hoping that things will change? We should look at ourselves that same way, as we continue to support the key players in America's two-party political system. It is time we plan and execute a mass exodus

from the Democratic Party and the sweet

nothings that they whisper every few years

to turn us on. It is time to stop groveling for

the validation of a party to whom we are

invisible, the Republican Party (GOP).

It is time to begin finding candidates

that look and think like us and have values

that align with the Green Party. We need to

put these people in office, at every level.

Turn the school boards green. Turn the

county commissions and city councils green.

Put some green in our state legislatures and

on our ballots. It does not make sense that California be the only state that has continuously recognized the Green Party presence and elected Green Party officials. The Green Party presents the most immediate option for Black America to consolidate their political party and magnify the collective's voice.

# Conclusion

Although I have only been able to
find one Black person in the entire movie,
one of my favorite holiday movies is *It's a
Wonderful Life* (1946).  The reason that I
appreciate the move so much is because it is
a tale of a community in which like-minded
people are concentrated in a specific locale,
everyone knows each other, and with one
exception is willing to help everyone else.
In the fictitious town of Bedford Falls, the
people have relationships with business
owners who they faithfully patronize, and
the town has a savings and loan bank that is

the center of the community. This provides

the perfect model for how a Black

community could operate, if they embraced

the cooperative segregation model that has

been discussed in this book.

In the perfect world the church

would be at the center and function as a

meeting place to discuss community

concerns and be the savings and loans bank.

Imagine if we after bringing tithes and

offerings to the church so that there was

meat, and members could actually access the

meat in the storehouse when needed.  I

digress.

In this not-so-perfect world in which

we have to chant "Black lives matter" in

order for some of us to even believe that

they do, there is a real solution.  It is a

cooperative segregation through which we

concentrate and consolidate financially,

geographically, and politically.  It is a model

through which we focus inward instead of

outward, on what we can do for ourselves

instead of what is being done to us.  It is a

model in which we stop trying to find peace

and success in a system that was not built for our peace and success. This model is an opportunity for Black Americans to reestablish dignity, self-respect, respect for each other, and free ourselves from the dependent status. This model could possibly even he the Americanized African gain the respect of the system that has abused us, exploited us, and resumed killing us at high rates.

# About the Author

**Marcus Johnson** is a collegiate English instructor, writer, consultant, mentor to at-risk youth, and an aficionado of politics, social science, and various genres of literature.  In addition to wearing these hats, he is also a dedicated worker within his religious community.  Although he has spent the majority of his life in metro Atlanta, Georgia, he still claims Palmyra, Virginia as his hometown.  Unlike the poetry and short stories that he has self-published and had published in literary magazines, Marcus's first nonfiction work – *Concentrated*

62

*Blackness* – has been driven by an intense love for his people and by a desire to share what he identifies as critical steps to the self-determinism of those people.